BRAD '61

BRAD

'61

PORTRAIT OF THE ARTIST AS A YOUNG MAN

AN ORIGINAL ROMANCE BY
TONY HENDRA
INSPIRED BY THE POP PAINTINGS OF
ROY LICHTENSTEIN

A BOB ADELMAN BOOK

PANTHEON BOOKS 🏛 NEW YORK

LIBRARY OF CONGRESS CATALOGING-IN-PUBLICATION DATA

LICHTENSTEIN, ROY, 1923–
BRAD '61 :
PORTRAIT OF THE ARTIST AS A YOUNG MAN
/ TONY HENDRA
P.   CM.
"A BOB ADELMAN BOOK."
ISBN 0-679-43097-0
1. LICHTENSTEIN, ROY, 1923–
2. ARTISTS' BOOKS—UNITED STATES.
3. POP ART—UNITED STATES.
I. HENDRA, TONY.   II. TITLE.
N7433.4.L53B73   1994
741.5'973—DC20   93-5614
CIP

MANUFACTURED IN ITALY BY EBS, VERONA
FIRST EDITION
9 8 7 6 5 4 3 2 1

IN NEW YORK CITY THINGS ARE HAPPENING

A NEW KIND OF ART IS

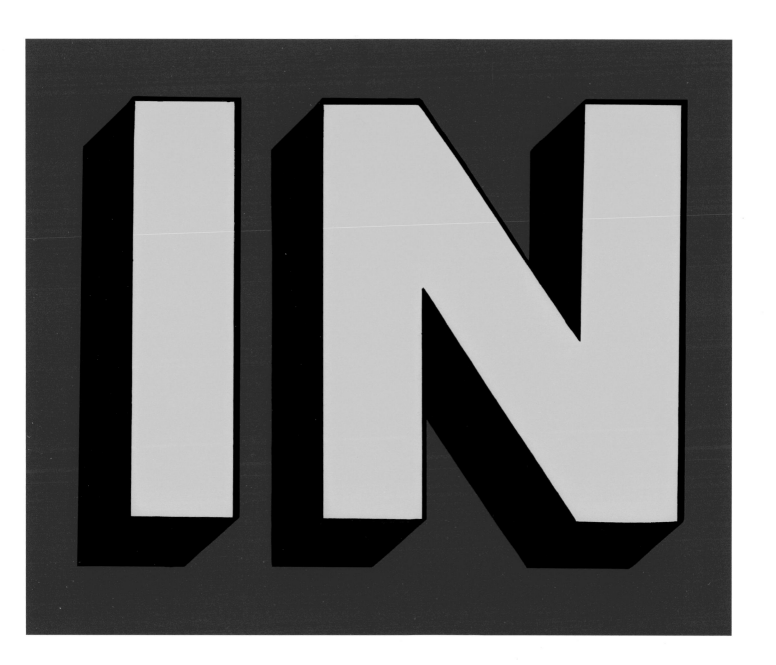

7

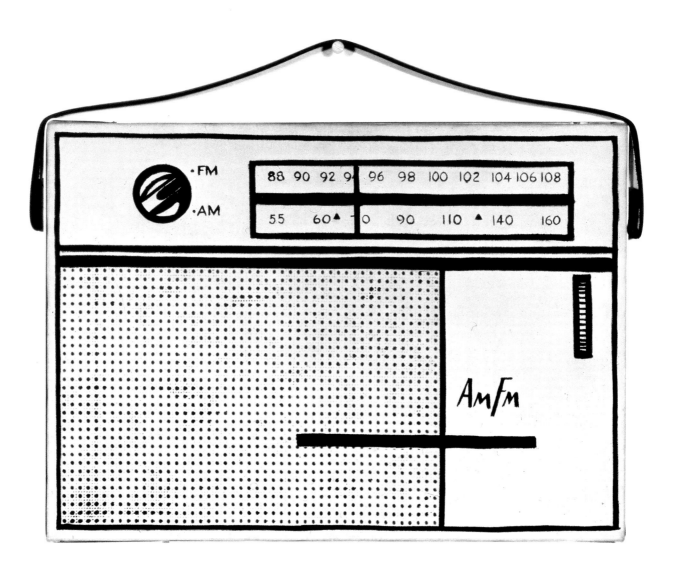

A NEW DAY
IS DAWNING

BUT NOT FOR **BRAD**

BRAD IS
AN ARTIST

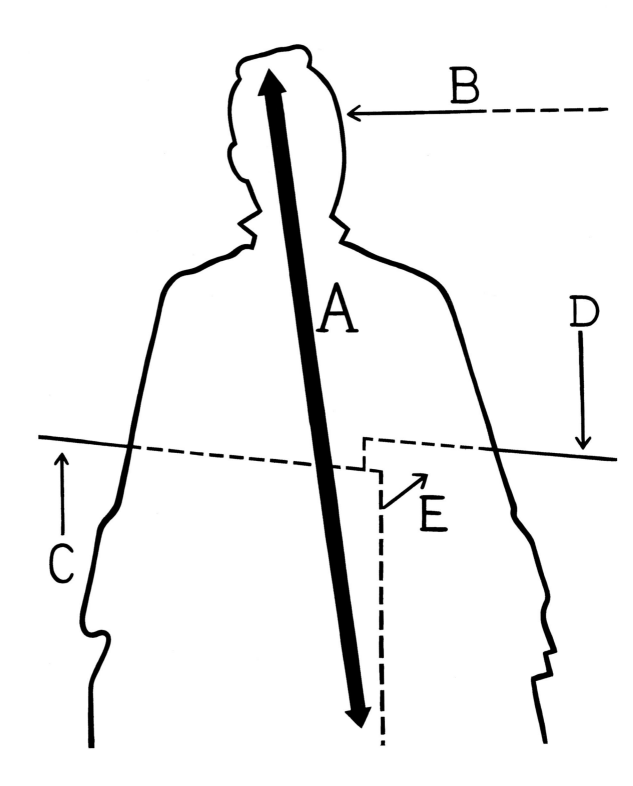

BUT THE ONLY WORK HE CAN GET IS ILLUSTRATING THE YELLOW PAGES

APPLIANCES . . .

FOODS: FROZEN—RETAIL . . .

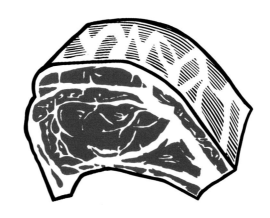

FOODS: READY TO SERVE . . .

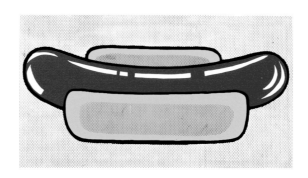

FOOTWEAR . . .

KITCHEN PRODUCTS . . .

SODA FOUNTAINS . . .

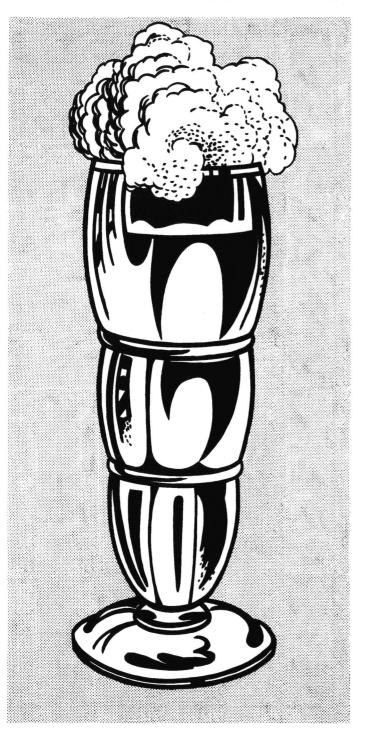

SPORTING GOODS . . .

IT'S HARDLY

FORGEDDABOUDIT!

HE TRIPPED OVER THE PLASTIC FLAMINGO ON HER LAWN

IT'S ENOUGH TO MAKE HIM CONTEMPLATE . . .

SUICIDE

UNKNOWN TO BRAD, HE _IS_ LOVED . . .

SHE THINKS ABOUT HIM ALL THE TIME—

EVEN WHEN SHE'S GETTING READY FOR WORK . . .

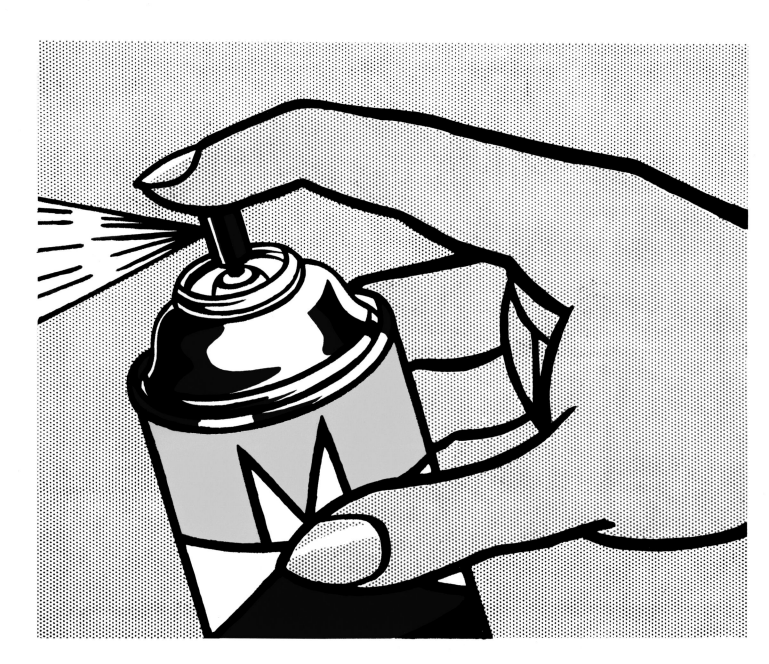

AT THE

DEW DROP INN

ON ROUTE 22

BRAD KNOWS NOTHING OF VICKI'S LOVE

HE HAS TO MAKE DO WITH HIS FANTASIES

51

53

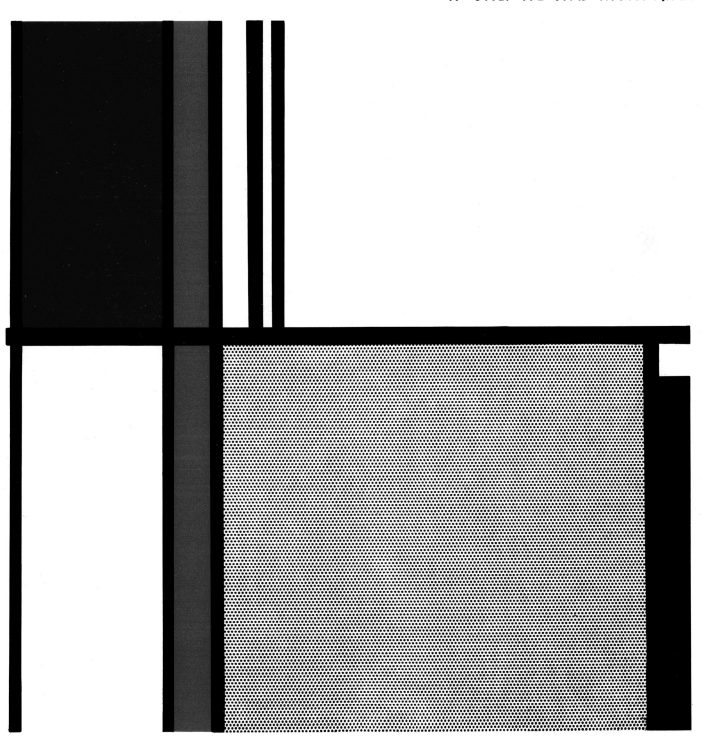

IF ONLY HE WAS MONDRIAN

THEN HE
COULD GET
A GIRL!

BRAD IS SURE HE'S A FAILURE

WHAT IS

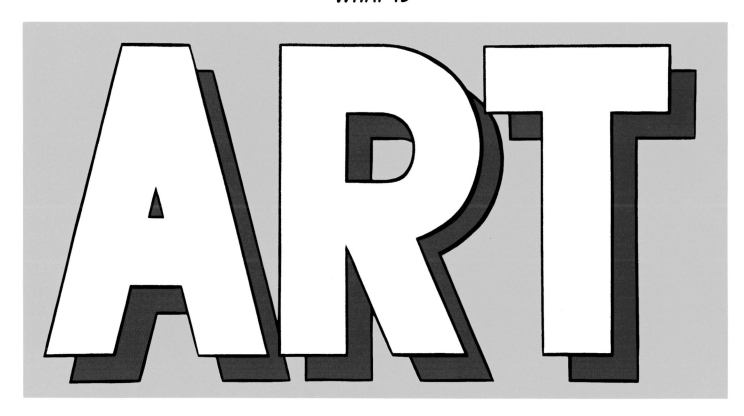

WHEN IS A MARK

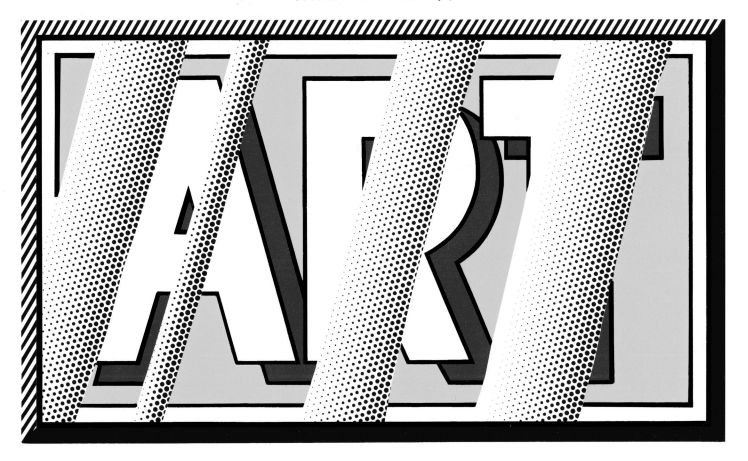

AND WHEN ISN'T IT?

WHEN BRAD GETS TO THINKING LIKE THIS HE LETS OFF STEAM

HE PAINTS
CUTE GIRLS IN
DUMB ADS

IN FACT HE'LL PAINT JUST ABOUT ANYTHING . . .

ONE DAY IN THE SPRING OF 1961 BRAD MAKES A DECISION.

HE'LL TAKE THE HUDSON TUBES TO MANHATTAN AND FIND AN ART EXPERT

LEO CASTELLI OR SOMEONE

AND ASK HIM: IS THIS

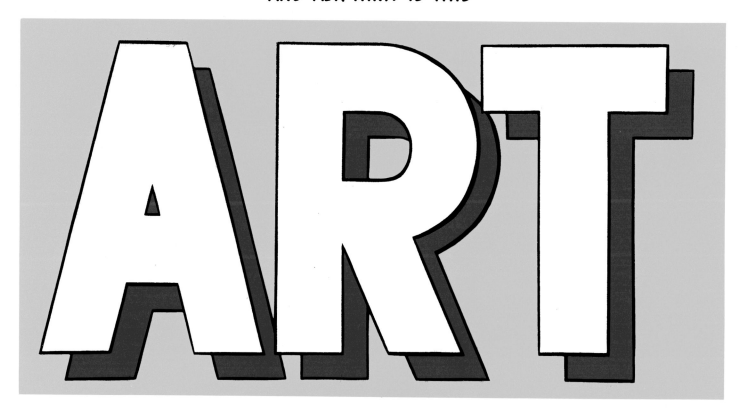

SUDDENLY

HE IS LOOKING

DOWN THE BARREL

OF A GUN

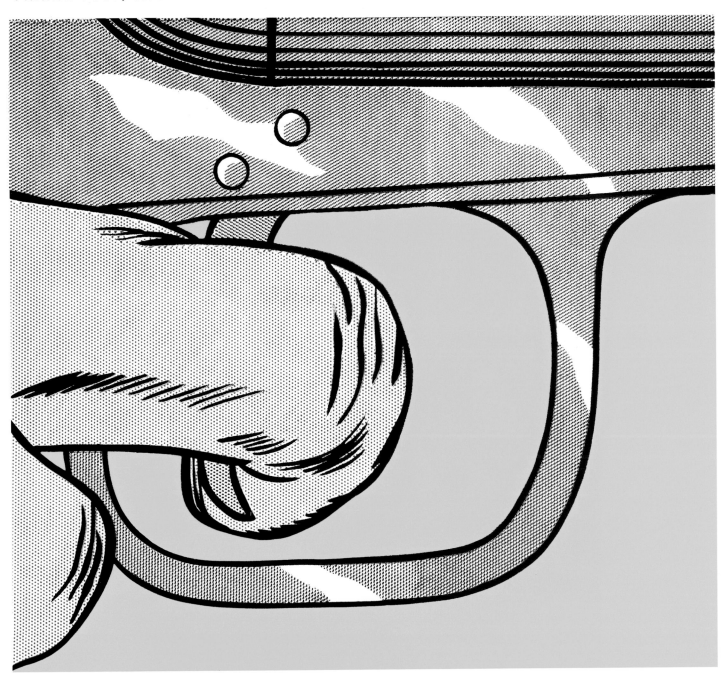

OUCH!

BRAD IS DEVASTATED.

IT'S A SIGN

HE WAS NEVER MEANT TO GO TO MANHATTAN

HE WAS NEVER MEANT TO FIND LEO CASTELLI OR SOMEONE

AND ASK HIM "IS THIS ART?"

SHE HEARS HIM STUMBLE THROUGH HIS DOOR AND CRIES OUT . . . !

THEIR LIPS MEET . . .

IT'S JUST THE WAY SHE THOUGHT IT WOULD BE . . .

WE ROSE UP SLOWLY ... AS IF WE DIDN'T BELONG TO THE OUTSIDE WORLD ANY LONGER ...LIKE SWIMMERS IN A SHADOWY DREAM ... WHO DIDN'T NEED TO BREATHE...

AFTERWARDS
VICKI WHISPERS
THAT SHE
CAN'T BELIEVE
THIS IS FINALLY
TRUE LOVE

SUDDENLY
IT HITS HIM
LIKE A
THUNDERBOLT

HIS LIFE IS A COMIC!   HIS LOVE IS A COMIC!   HIS ART IS A COMIC!

FEVERISHLY HE WORKS THROUGH THE NIGHT DRAWING THIS BOOK.

AT DAWN HE WAKES VICKI AND SHOWS IT TO HER

P.S. THEY LIVED HAPPILY EVER AFTER

Fin

LIST OF PLATES

44: HOPELESS, 1963
Oil on canvas
44 × 44
The Ludwig Collection
Wallraf-Richartz Museum,
Cologne

45: GIRL, 1963
Lithograph
16³⁄₁₆ × 11³⁄₄

46: SPRAY II, 1963
Oil on canvas
30 × 36
Private Collection

47: GIRL AT PIANO, 1963
Magna on canvas
68 × 48
Private Collection

48: GOOD MORNING,
DARLING, 1964
Magna on canvas
27 × 36
Private Collection

50

51: WHAAM!, 1963
Magna on canvas
2 panels, 68 × 166 total
The Tate Gallery, London

52: OKAY, HOT-SHOT!, 1963
Oil on canvas
80 × 68
Private Collection

53: THE KISS, 1961
Oil on canvas
80 × 67¼
Private Collection

54: STILL LIFE AFTER
PICASSO, 1964
Magna on plexiglass
48 × 60
Private Collection

55: NON-OBJECTIVE II, 1964
Magna on canvas
48 × 48
Private Collection

56: KISS III, 1962
Oil on canvas
64 × 48
Private Collection

58: ART, 1962
Oil on canvas
36 × 68
Private Collection

59: REFLECTIONS: ART, 1988
Oil and magna on canvas
44¼ × 76¼
Private Collection

61: GIRL WITH BALL, 1961
Oil and synthetic polymer
paint on canvas
60½ × 36½
The Museum of Modern Art,
New York

62: DROWNING GIRL, 1962
Oil on canvas
68 × 68
The Museum of Modern Art,
New York

63: FORGET IT!
FORGET ME!, 1962
Oil and magna on canvas
80 × 68
Brandeis University,
Rose Art Museum

64: ARTIST'S STUDIO
WITH MODEL, 1974
Oil and magna on canvas
96 × 128
Private Collection

65: FASTEST GUN, 1963
Magna on canvas
36 × 68
Private Collection

66: IMAGE DUPLICATOR, 1963
Magna on canvas
24 × 20
Private Collection

67: STRETCHER FRAME WITH
CROSS BARS III, 1968
Oil and magna on canvas
48 × 56
Private Collection

69: FEMME DANS UN
FAUTEUIL, 1963
Magna on canvas
68 × 48
Private Collection

70: BLAM, 1962
Oil on canvas
68 × 80
Private Collection

71: ALOHA, 1962
Oil on canvas
68 × 68
Private Collection

72: BRUSHSTROKES, 1965
Oil and magna on canvas
48 × 48
Private Collection

74: ART, 1962
Oil on canvas
36 × 68
Private Collection

75: HALF FACE WITH
COLLAR, 1963
Magna on canvas
48 × 48
Private Collection

76: PISTOL, 1964
Felt banner
82 × 49
Private Collection

77: TRIGGER FINGER, 1963
Oil and magna on canvas
36 × 40
Private Collection

78: SWEET DREAMS BABY!, 1965
Screenprint
37⅝ × 27⅝

79: EXPLOSION, 1965
Oil and magna on canvas
56 × 48
Private Collection

81: BLONDE WAITING, 1964
Magna on canvas
48 × 48
Private Collection

82: M-MAYBE, 1965
Oil and magna on canvas
60 × 60
The Ludwig Collection
Wallraf-Richartz Museum,
Cologne

83: CRYING GIRL, 1963
Offset Lithograph
18 × 24

84: VICKI, 1964
Enamel on steel
42 × 42
Private Collection

85: CRYING GIRL, 1964
Enamel on steel
46 × 46
Private Collection

86: KISS V, 1964
Magna on canvas
36 × 36
Private Collection

87: WE ROSE UP SLOWLY, 1964
Oil and magna on canvas
2 panels, 68 × 24 and 68 × 68
Frankfurt Museum of Modern Art

88: IT IS . . . WITH ME, 1963
Magna on canvas
34 × 24
Private Collection

89: SLEEPING GIRL, 1964
Magna on canvas
36 × 36
Private Collection

90: THUNDERBOLT, 1968
Felt banner
101 × 44½
Private Collection

91: MASTERPIECE, 1962
Oil on canvas
54 × 54
Private Collection

93: THE RING, 1962
Oil on canvas
48 × 70
Private Collection